Your Child Says, "I'm Gay"

Tim Geiger

New Growth Press

www.newgrowthpress.com

New Growth Press, Greensboro, NC 27404
www.newgrowthpress.com
Copyright © 2013 by Harvest USA

All Scripture quotations, unless otherwise indicated are from *The
Holy Bible, English Standard Version*® (ESV®), copyright © 2000,
2001 by Crossway Bibles, a division of Good News Publishers.
Used by permission. All rights reserved.

Scripture quotations marked NIV are taken from the *Holy Bible,
New International Version*®, NIV®. Copyright © 1973, 1978,
1984, 2011 by Biblica, Inc. Used by permission. All rights reserved
worldwide.

Cover Design: Faceout books, faceout.com
Typesetting: Lisa Parnell, lparnell.com

ISBN-10: 1-939946-03-4
ISBN-13: 978-1-939946-03-4

Library of Congress Cataloging-in-Publication Data
Geiger, Tim, 1968–
  Your child says, I'm gay / Tim Geiger. — 1st [edition].
     pages cm
  Includes bibliographical references and index.
  ISBN 978-1-939946-03-4 (alk. paper)
  1. Homosexuality—Religious aspects—Christianity. 2. Parent
and child—Religious aspects—Christianity. I. Title.
  BR115.H6G45 2013
  261.8'35766—dc23   2013024387

Printed in Canada

21 20 19 18 17 16 15 14   2 3 4 5 6

"I think I'm gay." Ed and Marie felt their hearts stop for an instant as everything around them seemed to stand still. It was like the shock of hearing that someone close to you has suddenly died. As they heard these words from their oldest son, Mark, twenty years old and home from college on spring break, Ed and Marie wondered whether this was also a kind of death for them—the death of their hopes and dreams for Mark, and the death of a life that had seemed safe and familiar.

Emma belonged to her local high school's Gay-Straight Alliance chapter, but she didn't tell her parents. When one of her friends let it slip, her parents confronted her. Then Emma exploded in defensiveness and blurted out, "I'm a lesbian, okay?"

Mark's and Emma's parents were in shock. They didn't know; they didn't realize. Now all sorts of questions flooded their minds. *Was this something* they *were responsible for? What will this mean for their children's future? Will they ever change? How will they deal with their "companions" if they wanted to spend the holidays with them? What would their friends at church say? What would grandparents and other family members say? Worse yet, what would they think—about Mark and Emma and about them as parents?* They wanted to ask questions. They wanted to tell their children they loved them. They wanted to convince their children that they were not what they thought they were. But Mark's and Emma's parents found themselves saying very little. The best they could do was try to take in their child's words: "I think I'm gay."

If you are a mother or father like these parents, you know the shock of such an admission. Or maybe you are a parent who suspects your son or daughter might have same-sex attraction (SSA) leanings. Maybe you have discovered gay pornography on your child's computer or smartphone. How do you respond? Not just in the moment, but after the shock begins to wear off and you try to move forward. What if you don't have words to describe the pain or know what to say to your child?

No Easy Answers

Your first instinct may be to find refuge in denial or anger. You may want to run from the situation, or you may find yourself angry—either at your child or at God. This is not what you expected in your life! You brought your child up in the church, as a follower of Jesus Christ. He attended church with you, involved himself in youth group, showed signs of spiritual growth. And now this. Who has wounded you the most, your child or God?

This is an understandable reaction. There are no easy answers to the "bombshells" that explode unexpectedly in your life. The first thing to do in the midst of your confusion is grab an anchor. That anchor is God—the One who promises that his love endures forever during all the changes. No matter how you may feel about him right now, go to him and pour out your troubles to him. Remember what God says to us when we encounter deep waters and believe that he will get you through this. "For I am the LORD your God who takes hold of your right hand and says to you, Do not fear; I will help you" (Isaiah 41:13 NIV). Keep going to God and asking for the help you need. Make that your morning and evening prayer—and your prayer anytime during the day when you feel overcome by confusion, grief, and fear.

With the knowledge that God is with you in this, even though you might be in turmoil, how do you respond to the announcement of your child being gay? There are a few key things to keep in mind as you try to help get through the difficult initial days or weeks after hearing this news.

You don't need to know all the answers

Don't feel as though you need to have all the answers right now, or even know all the questions to ask. It's okay to tell your child after his or her initial disclosure, "This is a lot to think about and take in. I need some time to think over what you've said. I'd like to sit down with you to talk about this in more depth later—after I've had some time to process and reflect."

It's also okay to feel upset and rattled inside. That would be a completely normal response, but now is a crucial time to watch your words. You can say that the news is upsetting; you don't need to stoically put on a good face and pretend that you are above feeling deeply impacted by this news. But simply letting loose your pain, fear, and anger will only complicate and compromise your ability to help your child. Proverbs 10:19 says, "When words are many, transgression is not lacking, but whoever restrains his lips is prudent." Pray earnestly for grace to choose your words wisely.

If the initial conversation has already taken place and you were not able to rein in your emotions, don't despair! You now have the opportunity to model humility and repentance to your child. Go to her and ask forgiveness.

Between the disclosure and the next time you talk with your child, prayerfully consider what questions you might ask. Ask your spouse, a trusted friend, or a pastor to help you think through some questions to ask and write them down. Use this time to process your emotions before God. He was not surprised by your child's news, and he can help you find peace and hope while you struggle to make sense of things. Your child was in charge of the initial disclosure, and he has probably been thinking about what he would say on this day for many weeks, months, or even years. So you don't have to quickly respond. Don't be rushed. Go at your own speed.

But make sure you are the one to make the effort and time to get back to your child. You might be tempted to let this painful issue slide for a while. It will be hard to face this and to start a dialogue about it with your child, but you must. Just as God did not abandon or leave us alone in our struggles and sin, but sent his Son to step into the brokenness of our lives to redeem us, we do the same. We step into our children's lives with love even when we know that our children don't agree with our perspective. "But God shows his love for us in that while we were still sinners, Christ died for us" (Romans 5:8). Even though the news your child gave you was perhaps the last thing you wanted to hear, she honored you and her relationship with you by telling you the truth. Reciprocate and give back to her the gift of honesty about yourself and what you believe to be true.

Acknowledge the courage it took to tell you

Most likely your child has been struggling with this issue in silence for a long time. By not acknowledging this fact, they have contributed to a "pretense" relationship with you. The odds are good they didn't want that, but they were afraid to bring this out in the open for fear of your response or how it would impact you. So even if this news is devastating to you, acknowledge to your child how hard it must have been to both keep it secret and to finally get it out in the open. At least by acknowledging the truth, you can help your child in this journey and you can relate to each other authentically. God is the author of all truth, so accepting the truth about someone you love is a great first step in seeing what God can do.

Affirm your love for your child

No matter what ultimately happens, no matter what your son or daughter says, feels, or does, he or she is still your child. Express your love for her. Promise her that there's nothing that would ever cause you to withhold that love. This may be difficult to do, but the most important way parents can minister to their child who has adopted a gay identity is to keep the lines of communication open and the relationship going. Your child's behavior may not be direct rebellion against you, although if there is anger in her declaration you will most likely be the prime recipient of that anger. Keep in mind that your child's struggle with her sexuality is primarily an issue with God. Your child is either confused about or opposed to what God says about homosexuality in the Scriptures. It is important not to take this as an attack on you personally. Maintaining contact with your child and continuing to love her as you have always done is the best way to witness to her the Lord's unfailing and faithful love in her life. Psalm 73 describes a struggle the psalmist had with God and how at one time his heart was embittered toward him.

When my soul was embittered,
    when I was pricked in heart,
I was brutish and ignorant;
    I was like a beast toward you.

Nevertheless, I am continually with you;
    you hold my right hand.
You guide me with your counsel. . . ."
    (Psalm 73:21–24)

Begin the dialogue

By adopting a grace-filled and compassionate response toward your child after the disclosure, the door is open to enter into his life and struggle redemptively. By not going on the offensive or immediately lecturing your child on why what they are doing is wrong, you will help to defuse his normal defensiveness to hearing what you have to say. Your child likely knows your position, and he expects that to be your first salvo. But now is the time for discussion and dialogue. Continuing to build your relationship is the foundation that may eventually allow your child to hear what at this time he will not or cannot hear. To be life-changing, truth must come wrapped in the arms of love for the person you want to reach.

Use this time to ask good follow-up questions about his life. What is going on in the bigger picture of his life, and what are his hopes for the future in light of his disclosure? There is a whole lot of "background" information to learn about your child here (after all, there was a lot hidden before this), and you want to help him move toward being increasingly open and honest with you.

It's important to ask your child what he means by saying he is gay. Don't take for granted that your child's understanding of the terms he uses to describe himself is the same as yours. Ask your child how he came to this conclusion, how long has he been thinking about it, how certain he feels it is true, and why.

You may find that your child isn't so much making a statement about his identity as giving his assessment of a situation in which he perceives himself as helpless. He might really be saying, "I've been struggling with these feelings for years, and the only reasonable conclusion I can draw is that I must be gay." Saying you're gay and saying you've been wrestling with feelings you don't understand and don't want are two completely different things. Our world says that if you feel attraction to your gender, then you're gay. There's no further debate. This can be premature, especially if your child is in his or her teen years, which is when one's sexuality is still being formed and there is often confusion about identity. You don't want to be in denial if your child is experiencing same-sex attraction, but you also do not want to rush forward and agree with your child's label that he is gay—a label the surrounding culture would certainly use.

Ask whether your child has fully embraced this new identity or whether he is open to explore other options. If he is willing to discuss this, here are some suggestions for several conversations that can be helpful over time:

1. If he professes to be a Christian or is willing to listen to God's perspective, talk about the role of Christian faith. Don't lead the discussion at this time toward calling your child to repent and change. The Christian faith is more than just throwing Bible verses at different situations in life. It's about a relationship with Jesus Christ, and in that relationship God works deeply and patiently over time. Your life of faith will be the most powerful demonstration to your child of what it really means to trust and obey God through the ups and downs of life.

How do you begin to talk about faith without coming across as judgmental? One way is to share with your child that the fundamental Christian perspective on the world is that it is broken and fallen, and that what "is" is not the way things should be. Even the good things of God's creation are bent and broken in many ways. As we try to make sense of life and all its struggles, our hearts naturally make something other than God central. We cling to idols that we believe will help us get what we think we need for life apart from God—approval, acceptance, power, pleasure, comfort, safety—the list is endless. And we make central in our life a way to deal with the pain we experience in this broken world. This is the essence of sin: looking to and embracing something (a person, a career, possessions, a way of life, a behavior like alcohol or drug abuse or sexual promiscuity, etc.), rather than turning to God and clinging to him for meaning and purpose in life. Idols are God substitutes, and often the strongest and most powerful idols are relational.

2. This might also be a good time for you to talk about the role of feelings, desires, and hopes in your own life, and how trusting Jesus brings his help into your life. Give illustrations from your own life of how, by faith, you can keep following Jesus when you are confused, struggling, or even angry at God. The attraction of homosexuality comes out of a God-given desire in everyone to be in relationship with someone. But in a broken and fallen world, not everyone will be able to be in a marriage relationship as God designed it to be (between one man and one woman), either through broken sexuality (like SSA) or through simply not finding someone. There are many

hopes and dreams in life that are not going to be realized. For those with SSA who choose to follow Scripture, they may find themselves in turmoil like Peter, who wondered if it really was worth it to follow Jesus and leave many good things behind in life.

In Mark 10:28–30, we hear the gracious words of Christ to us in the midst of times when our desires conflict with what faith must choose.

> Peter began to say to him, "See, we have left everything and followed you." Jesus said, "Truly, I say to you, there is no one who has left house or brothers or sisters or mother or father or children or lands, for my sake and for the gospel, who will not receive a hundredfold now in this time, houses and brothers and sisters and mothers and children and lands, with persecutions, and in the age to come eternal life."

To follow Jesus means not only the loss of those things that our hearts may want (and about which the world says, "You can/should have it!"); it also means that Jesus will give us untold numbers of blessings—in this life and in the one to come. When Jesus says that we will receive "a hundredfold" of blessings in this life, his words are meant to exaggerate this fact: you will not be able to comprehend the richness and the depth of your life when you give yourself over completely to follow him and his word. This is a truth that anyone experiencing SSA needs to hear and believe because our culture asserts that failure to embrace a gay identity and life is false and tragic.

3. You can also discuss with your child the dominant "voice" of the culture today and how its message may seem appealing, but it is, in fact, full of chaos and confusion. We live in a sexually chaotic world where traditional boundary lines are being erased. Views about sex are a contradiction today. On the one hand, sex is considered to be nothing more than any other human activity, like eating and drinking, so why shouldn't someone engage in it when the need, the desire, or the occasion seems to warrant it. On the other hand, sex is seen as the penultimate human experience. Sex equals life, and a life without sex is seen today as abnormal, as a major tragedy. Sex is elevated above all other human activity, rather than being seen as just one part of life or better yet, one part of a marriage relationship. From a casual "just do it" to an anxious "I must have it," sex today is completely out of balance. The result of these wildly inconsistent messages is to leave both parents and youth confused about sexuality. Rather than turning to Scripture for answers, youth are turning to their peers and to famous media personalities to help resolve their concerns and struggles. And the message they hear is, "If you feel this way, then this is who you are, so embrace it—go with it."

There is something about what is happening here in the culture surrounding sex that echoes the biblical accounts. It is the voice of men and women who are made in the image of God, proclaiming rebellion against God's design. That is the definition of sin: proclaiming independence and autonomy from God and his ways. It is an embrace of brokenness, disguised as freedom and self-fulfillment.

4. Ask your child if he is content to be gay, or if this is something he really doesn't want. Some children will quickly state they're happy—and if your child does, you likely won't be able to convince him otherwise. Others may report years of inner turmoil, guilt, and shame over their feelings and behavior and will express either desire to change or questions about whether that is possible. If so, enter into that struggle by sensitively talking to him. Point out the difference between identifying oneself as someone who has same-sex attraction (SSA) from someone who describes his identity as being gay. To base one's identity on being gay is something quite different from acknowledging attraction to the same sex. Accepting gay as an identity can move one to import all the cultural expectations and associations connected with that identity, and that can be problematic for someone who wishes to align his sexuality within a biblical framework.

5. If your child seems open to more input, ask if he or she is willing to talk to someone about this, like their pastor, youth pastor, or a Christian counselor. This doesn't mean you are going to step out of this discussion entirely, but your child may feel

more comfortable talking about issues of sexuality with someone other than their parents. Here it is ***crucial*** to help him select a Christian counselor whose faith position is solidly scriptural, who understands issues of sexuality and youth, and who will help him explore what it would mean for him to align his decisions about who he feels he is with scriptural principles.

6. Study and read together (if she is willing to examine this issue with you). Ask your child to look at materials that explain her position—so you can better understand it and can better understand how to talk with her about it. This may mean that you need to be prepared to read materials that take an unbiblical view of homosexuality, especially those that proclaim a new understanding of Scripture on the subject. If this is what your child is reading and has become convinced of (and maybe she has begun attending a gay-affirming church that further supports her position), you need to study to find out how their conclusions are reached. Then, find some well-written materials you can explore together that present a biblical and compassionate perspective on homosexuality and the gospel. There is a short resource list at the end of this minibook.

But keep this in mind: after some conversations, your child may not want to talk about this issue any longer. You must respect this. If every time you are with your child the topic centers on SSA, it will likely push him away from you.

At some point, it will be important for you to ask for permission to talk about this issue again, while assuring him that every conversation won't revolve around SSA issues.

You don't need to know details about your child's sexual activity

If your child is over eighteen this information is often not beneficial for a parent to know, and may serve only to separate you from your child. It is okay to ask general questions. "Are you in a relationship? With whom? Who else knows?"

If your child is under eighteen, then it is important to ascertain some level of detail about his or her behavior. "Are you acting on your sexual attractions? How so (is what you feel limited to fantasy and masturbation)? Is pornography involved? Have you had sexual contact with anyone?" Keep in mind that these kinds of questions can be difficult for you to ask and for your child to hear. Here, again, it may be wise to enlist the services of a good Christian counselor, one who can help you learn not only how to talk to your child about these sensitive matters, but who, because he or she is outside the family, might better relate to your child in asking these sensitive questions.

Also, in the case of a minor, it is important to assess the situation and determine if laws have been broken and if your child is at risk from a predator, either in person or online. It is also essential to determine if sexual abuse has occurred, and if so to report this to law enforcement as quickly as possible. To determine how to proceed, talk to a counselor who is familiar with your state's laws about child sexual abuse.

You can't change your child

You cannot change your child. No matter how badly you might want to see change, no matter how much you pray, no matter how convincing your argument, you won't be able to convince your child to change. Your child's issue ultimately isn't with you; it's with God.

Only a transforming relationship with Jesus Christ will lead to the **heart change** that is needed before **behavioral change** will occur. God wants to do business with your child's heart. Your child has adopted a gay identity because, at some level, he has believed lies about God, himself, and others. Romans 1:21–25 is a clear and sobering description of human behavior in a broken and fallen world. Paul lays out an argument about how the knowledge and pursuit of God is suppressed and twisted in favor of believing lies about God and turning to idols to find life.

> For although they knew God, they did not honor
> him as God or give thanks to him, but they
> became futile in their thinking, and their foolish
> hearts were darkened. Claiming to be wise, they
> became fools, and exchanged the glory of the
> immortal God for images resembling mortal
> man and birds and animals and creeping things.
> Therefore God gave them up in the lusts of their
> hearts to impurity, to the dishonoring of their

bodies among themselves, because they exchanged the truth about God for a lie and worshiped and served the creature rather than the Creator, who is blessed forever! Amen.

This is *not* a passage to hammer your child with about their same-sex attractions! Romans 1 isn't targeted merely to homosexuals. Paul is talking to all of us! He is saying that everyone in the world has been so impacted by the fall that we all are guilty of serious idolatry, and only a real, transforming relationship with Jesus Christ will enable us to live in increasing wholeness and godliness before God.

Use this passage to remind yourself that, while you can work toward being an agent of change in your child's life, you can't expect that you will be able to convince your child to change or make him change. It's only the Lord who does the changing in our lives. Such change is likely to come about over time, within the context of Christian community—through your relationship with your son or daughter and through his or her relationship with other mature, compassionate Christians who are willing to walk with those who struggle with SSA and not abandon them through this journey.

Your child doesn't need to become straight

Your child's deepest need is not to become straight. Your child's deepest need is the same as every person in this world—a life of faith and repentance in Christ. Having heterosexual sex will not solve your child's problem. There is more to this issue than sexuality. The ethical opposite of homosexuality is not "becoming straight." Godly sexuality is about holiness. It is about living out one's sexuality by increasingly being willing to conform and live within God's design for sex. Godly sexuality is not merely about being heterosexual; it is not merely about being married and having two kids and living in the suburbs.

Godly sexuality also includes being single and celibate, refusing to be controlled by one's sexual desires because one chooses to follow a higher value in one's life—to follow God even when it's not easy or popular (particularly in the area of sexuality today). Rich relationships and friendships are possible and achievable for singles. Again, the world will have us believe that a life without sex is tragic and not "true to yourself," but Jesus and the witness of the New Testament is evidence against that false worldview.

Being celibate today is not an easy road. If your son or daughter chooses to follow God's design for sexuality by remaining celibate, they will need to find people who will support that decision and help them live a godly life. But celibacy may not be the only path that is open before them. There are some men and women who, in turning away from a gay-identified life, have found a fulfilling marriage relationship with the opposite sex. Over time, many have found a lessening of SSA desires and some have even found growth in heterosexual desires (most often not in a general sense, but toward a specific person with whom they have grown to love).

In other words, it is important to bring multiple stories of transformation and change to the discussion. You do not know what the Lord has in store for your child's future. Marriage may be out of the question— for now and possibly for the future. Waiting upon the Lord and seeking his will and wisdom is what is needed, and that will be the faith journey your child will have to walk.

Your child's struggle with homosexuality is something the Lord means for your good

You may still feel anger toward God, but now is the time to hold on to what you know of him. He is sovereign, and he is good. He knows what you are going through, and he is strong and tender enough to handle your pain. Allow God's Word to be an anchor for your turbulent emotions. If we believe that God is sovereign and at work in each of his children in every circumstance (Philippians 2:12–13), then God intends this present situation as a means to grow you in faith and dependence upon him. This may be hard to believe right now, but it is the direction your faith in him needs to go. Ask him to help you get there.

You can't do anything to manipulate or control your child's struggle or repentance. You can, however, respond to what the Lord is calling you to do in terms of faith, obedience, and repentance in your own life as you struggle with these issues in your family. Will you rest solely in God's love and sovereignty, or will you resort to trying to resolve these issues on your own, in a spirit of self-sufficiency?[1]

Bring others in

No matter how strong your faith, you can't deal with this on your own. Seek out trusted and spiritually mature friends, family members, church members, and pastors to help you both interpret the events in your family from a biblical perspective and to help you respond in a holy and God glorifying way to your child's decisions. God especially ministers to his people in the context of Christian community. Don't let your fears—of embarrassment, of what others might think—get in the way of allowing others to walk with you for support, prayer, and deep encouragement. Difficult though it might be to believe at the outset, God really does work all things together for good, to conform you to the image of Christ (Romans 8:28–29). God wants to transform your heart, as well as your child's, through this hard process. It is likely that the only way you'll see that transformation occur in you is to bring in others who are compassionate and wise friends.

If you think there is no one who can handle these issues, then pray. People you can trust are out there! Ask the Lord to open your eyes to see someone with whom you might speak. The Lord can raise up someone to walk with you—and frequently does—in response to prayer, though they may not be the people you expect. You might consider starting a parents' support group at your church. You are not alone in this struggle, and talking to, praying with, and walking alongside others in this journey is not only crucial, it can be another way God will bring much good out of your pain to others in the body of Christ.

You can also contact Harvest USA to ask about the "Shattered Dreams/New Hope Parents Intensive Seminar," designed to help parents exactly in your situation. The seminar will help you understand your situation in the context of God's Word and in community with God's people.

What about setting boundaries in my relationship with my child?

It may be appropriate to set some boundaries with your child if she or he lives in your home. Those boundaries will be unique for each family and will often change as needs and circumstances dictate. For example, if your child is in a relationship, you will find yourself needing to think through situations about your child and his partner that you never imagined facing. The tension between one's beliefs and one's relationships can be a difficult road to navigate.[2] Boundaries should exist to protect your family and your child, and they should be rules that reflect your own faith and ethics. Boundaries should never be punitive or manipulative. To be punitive or manipulative fails to reflect the faithful love of God through Jesus Christ, which should be the overarching principle of relationship with your child. Jesus uncompromisingly spoke the truth in love. We, as his disciples, can do nothing else.

Finally, pray. Pray for wisdom. Pray for faith. Pray for strength to reflect the love of God through Jesus Christ to your child. Keep the lines of communication open with your child. Make sure your child knows that he can always come to you. At the same time, give him space to make his own decisions. Respecting those decisions does not mean you agree with or condone them. There will be times you need to let your son or daughter realize the natural consequences of their behavior. If your child makes decisions to pursue self-destructive or otherwise sinful behavior, communicate to him the sinfulness of that decision and your disappointment—but do not withhold your love as punishment.

The Lord has sovereignly placed you in this situation with a son or daughter who is struggling with unbelief and sin in particular ways. Rest assured that he is at work in all things—especially the hard things—for the *good* of those who are called according to his purpose (Romans 8:28). He hasn't forgotten you. To the contrary, he is the only One capable of helping you grow in faith and hope in the midst of a dark and difficult time. Believe that he will!

A few resources to help you and your son or daughter think biblically about homosexuality. This is *not* an exhaustive list; it's only a few to help you get the dialogue going.

Black, Nicholas, ed. *Your Gay Child Says, "I Do."* Greensboro, NC: New Growth Press, 2012. A minibook from Harvest USA.

Dallas, Joe. *The Gay Gospel: How Pro-Gay Advocates Misread the Bible*. Eugene, Oregon: Harvest House, 2007.

Harvest USA staff. *Gay . . . Such Were Some of Us: Stories of Transformation and Change*. Greensboro, NC: New Growth Press. A collection of personal testimonies from those who lived a gay life and those who struggled with SSA and how their faith in Christ changed them.

Hill, Wesley. *Washed and Waiting, Reflections on Christian Faithfulness and Homosexuality.* Grand Rapids, MI: Zondervan, 2010. A personal and theological reflection that combines scriptural examination and Wesley's own personal journey.

White, David. *Can You Change If You're Gay?* Greensboro, NC: New Growth Press, 2013. A minibook from Harvest USA that addresses issues of change and sexual identity.

www.harvestusa.org. A Christian ministry that has helped men and women since 1983 deal with SSA in a Christian context. This website has many online resources that give a biblical and practical perspective on living well within God's design for sexuality.

Yarhouse, Mark A. *Homosexuality and the Christian: A Guide for Parents, Pastors and Friends.* Ada, MI: Bethany House, 2010. An excellent book to examine some of the latest issues about the origin of homosexuality, what options there are for Christians with SSA, and how family, the church, and friends can help.

Endnotes

1. Nicholas Black, ed., *Your Gay Child Says, "I Do"* (Greensboro, NC: New Growth Press, 2012) is an excellent minibook that lays out several (additional) ways parents can relate well to their gay child while growing in their own faith in Christ and holding onto a continued adherence to the Scriptures on issues of sexuality and change.

2. The minibook, *Your Gay Child Says "I Do,"* contains a number of boundary issues you will need to navigate.